# My Poetry is

# The Beauty You Overlook

# By Kim B Miller

i

# Dedication

I dedicate this book to poets. The overlooked word slayers who are often underappreciated and under paid.

# Table of Contents

# Poetry

I am not your definition of poetry

Poetry is not picture perfect and no, it will not fit into your mold

I'm not a performing seal, barking for your applause

I'm a writer, a creator of truth

I am your conscious screaming to be heard

I am the words you dare not speak

I am the truth you will not face

My name is poetry and I will never be what you want to hear

But truth cannot be ignored

Poetry is not what I do

Words are what I breathe and I decided to come exhale on you

# Haiku

Haiku

Poetry heals. I
don't think you heard me. This ain't
no game. It's a cure.

## Haiku (continued)

### Poetry
Dear poets don't let
another poet decide
how you spit your truth.

### Judging
Just cause they don't po-
et like you poet that doesn't
mean they aren't poets.

### Chris Browning
How can you have mad,
hate outside of the poem? You
can't even get in.

### Read
Stop judging poets
who read their poems. You don't de-
cide who's relevant.

### COVID
The virus came. Po-
ets buried snaps. No one came
to the funeral.

### Bars
Some of you are try-
ing to write "bars" but dope po-
ets keep raising it.

4

# Kimism

## I'm a Poet

**I didn't write this poem
so you
could like it.**

**I wrote this poem
so you
could hear it.**

KimBMiller.com

# Move
# Forward

When did you decide to take a backseat in your own life

You were never meant to live in your own shadow

I know that darkness can be enticing

Your comfort level secure

Your insecurities hidden

But you can't play hide and seek with pain

Pain will wait for you

Flaws are beauty marks on the road to greatness

Scars remind us that imperfections don't kill us

Missteps don't erase effort

But you can't succeed if you are transcribing judgement

Blinking in doubt

Hesitating instead of creating

If you feed sadness how will joy grow

Stop waiting for opportunity to knock

Go find her

Braille her with your vision

I'm not asking you to look at the glass as half full

I'm asking you to be grateful that you have something to drink

Think about it...

If you gave up every time you fell you wouldn't be walking now

Break out of your self-imposed isolation

You locked yourself in hoping solitude would breed success

But your purpose waits to be discovered

While you Netflix and chill your goals are going on HBO (Hope Basically Optional)

You made your situation your identity

You put a down payment on pain but rented solutions

You're in a relationship with hours when you need to be dating seconds

Don't beg time to stay

Just use what you have

Before time does, what it always does

Leave

# Haiku

## Be original

Haiku
You can copy some-

one's blueprint, but if it's not

their ink, it won't work!

KimBMiller.com

# Haiku (continued)

## Scared
It's okay to be
scared, do it anyway. Scared
people succeed too.

## See It
Please recognize your
accomplishments or you will
label them failures.

## Too Bright
If someone says you
shine too bright, tell them to take
a seat in your shade.

## Divide
You cannot divide
yourself into fractions to
make someone else whole

## Glow Stick
They thought they broke you
but you are a glow stick. They
just exposed your light.

## Fall
How many times do
you have to fall, before you
stop tripping yourself?

# Kimism

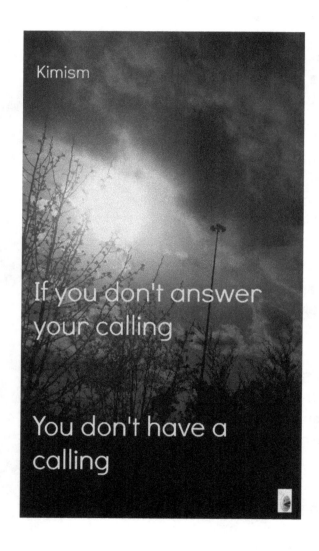

# Black Crayon

I wonder if the black crayon knows how it is pronounced in Spanish and treated in English

I wonder if the black crayon knows it was never meant to be colored with, only used

If it was discarded, it would be blamed for being un-useful

I wonder if the black crayon knows it is hated

I wonder if it knows it must stay in the corner of the box

Segregated from the better colors

Since it's too dark

Pigmentation challenged

Treated like a leaper

Looked at for problems but not solutions

Roasted like charcoal and blamed for the fire

I wonder if the black crayon knows if it broke

It would be blamed for being broken

While pretending to be whole

It will not scream

It will stand quietly, still

Hoping its color is not the cause of its own destruction

I wonder if the black crayon knows if it could not color anymore

It would still be called colored or lack with a b in front of it (black)

If it was chosen

It would be drawing something ugly

Watching its color being secured to anger

Begging for a chance to draw beauty

Black crayons repent for your misconceptions

When one black crayon draws outside the line every black crayon is answerable

Maybe they could try to look softer

Maybe their hardness is a protective coating

A black crayon can write in several languages and be ignored in all of them

Crayons grieve

I wonder how often black crayons cry

Can they hear their own tears drip or is solitude louder than pain

Will you draw black tears or just call them periods

Aren't sentences "syllable-zed" weapons that end with a black dot

I wonder if black crayons ever compare war stories with black pens

I wonder if a crayon can draw its own agony

With no paper willing to accept the weight of its thoughts

What are black crayons supposed to draw

Should they lightly sketch how loneliness permeates inside of a crowded box

This box is so small

Black crayons smell freedom each time the box is opened

They are taught discipline

They know their place

They draw whole or it pieces

They draw life and defy death

They bleed inside that box

Even when selected the black crayon knows it's only temporary air

After all boxes are not made to be empty

# Haiku

We are black butter-
flies, trying to get you to
see that we have wings

## Haiku (continued)

### Stand
You want Blacks to stand,
but you don't try to under-
stand, what we stand for.

### History
Well, it is Febru-
ary. Time for Blacks to be
history again.

### Movie
"Hidden Figures" should
be called Silent Strength; Lies You
Told, or Buried Truth.

### Martin
I had a dream that
Martin made more than just one
speech. Are you awake?

### Solution
Racism isn't a so-
lution to pain. Don't bleed on
those who didn't cut you.

### Comfort
We're sick of making
other people comforta-
ble, while we suffer.

# Kimism

Kimism

When a flower

dies,

the entire forest cries.

They don't check

the color

of the flower.

19

# Parents

I am not your excuse to make things right

I am not a living example for you to use

Why do you try so hard but do so little

I don't expect anything

I just want to exist in the same space you possess

But you are so busy

Busy doing things that make you important

Important to others

You need not perform for me

I don't want it

I want you to see me

I want you, to want to see me

No, I have no award

I'm not in a play

I just need your full vision for longer than a second

Look at me

Do not glance

Look at me

I want to matter to you

Don't rush pass me

Stop and sit

Make me matter

Make me yours

I am your child

Not a project that needs attention

Enjoy me now before I am gone

Growth and time will not hesitate to take me

Soon you will wonder

Where did the time go

It has not simply gone

You threw it away

The Corona virus gave you forced time

You use it begrudgingly

I was not a welcome sight, more like a burden

It took a virus to give you time that you didn't want

Trapped

Physically here but mentally ghost

Will you eventually embrace what we have

A second chance at a relationship we never started

Your excuses have left you

Don't make me join them

# Haiku

Haiku

Your son spends more time
with Fortnite than he does with
you. Toys don't raise kings.

# Haiku (continued)

## Grades
If you don't post when
they get a F, then don't post
when they get an A.

## Math
Your children don't know
their times table, but they know
they can't count on you.

## Pain
Never complain a-
bout how someone expresses
the pain that you caused.

## Daughters
Are we more conscious
of the ways we raise our daugh-
ters? No Nas, we aren't.

## Music
How do "they" get your
10 year old to twerk instead
of study? Music.

## Listen
If you believe their
bully then you're telling your
kid their pain isn't real.

# Kimism

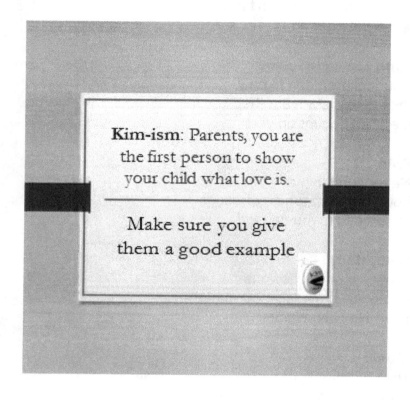

Kim-ism: Parents, you are the first person to show your child what love is.

Make sure you give them a good example

# Love

I hear the birds

I hear the happiness in their chirps

Their melody is floating on a stream of air and I inhaled

I am an admirer of beautiful things

I worship completeness

I don't grasp at compliments because I love the fragrance called me

There may be gaps in my teeth but not in my beauty

I see stretch marks as lines that allow me write on my soul

I love this feeling of completeness

I'm not a ray of light

I'm a burst of sunshine

I see courage in the cracks that people overlook

What you call broken, I call a masterpiece of unassembled pieces

The love that radiates from you

I feel it

I heed to your frequency

I don't judge your flow

I choose to see you, not critic you

I emancipate your baggage

I superimpose love on your hurt so I can see you better

I invite you to RSVP to contentment

Display more compassion

Drip anxious thoughts

Cleanse love

Create solutions to future problems

Love is free, don't hoard it

Outthink your selfishness

So love can be a resource

Expand

Swim in this deep end of love

No one can eclipse you

Love is not missing

It's soul deep

Look within

# Haiku

## Your biggest competition is you!

### Haiku

If you are <u>not</u> racing against yourself then you are on the wrong track.

KimBMiller.com

# Haiku (continued)

## Talking
Stop talking about
cutting people off. You know
your knife ain't that sharp.

## Blame
Some of you are blam-
ing yourself for being cut
by broken people.

## Escape
Escape their neglect
and watch hope exhale slowly.
Peace whispers you're safe.

## Fly
Just because they're in
your nest, that does not mean they
want to see you fly.

## Deep
If your pain runs deep
why is your response so shal-
low? Read that again.

## Joy
If you give them the
key to your joy, when they leave
they can take the lock.

# Kimism

Some of you are too busy trying to explain your journey to someone who will not be going with you.

KimBMiller.com

# Light

The separation between darkness and light is just a thin thread or a drop of infinity

Your perspective will pick which one is fluid for you

No language can translate agony

It is undefinable but the flavor is so recognizable

Like an old friend whose name you can't recall but whose face you can't forget

You let your intrusions violate your peace

You can't stop the avalanche you created but maybe you won't form another storm in your life

Aren't enough tragedies named after you

Look at the destruction, left in your wake

Aftershocks that trigger more agony

I walked in the storm that you left behind

I was soaked in disappointment

I was too intertwined to see my involvement

I let my mind manipulate you

I couldn't see the hurt that resided in your eyes

I wasn't humble enough to see it

I engulfed you in your past

You are allowed to blossom without my approval

You don't have to count pedals

A flower blinked once

Then a tear rolled down its stem, dying in a vase

I won't be the vase that steals you from your freedom

Your stem is beautifully formed to withstand my knife

I whispering to the softness of the wind

The wind answered

I saw the leaves falling at your feet

I knew I had to join them

I thought I was painting a picture of you when I actually painted the truth about me

You grow more beautiful everyday

The sweetness of you is like perfumed goodness

You're a flower that grew without natural light

I made the shadows your home

Impassable but you grew in a different way

I mourn the flowers that have withered away

I mourn the wrongs I cannot correct

No more flowers will die by my hand

I will be more cognizant of the petals that touch my hand

I will not starve growth

I want to…I want to see a sunset

Since the separation between darkness and light is just a thin thread or a drop of infinity

I want to experience infinity in the light

# Haiku

## Haiku (continued)

### Cry
My tears screamed catch me
but I was too busy catch-
ing you. Can tears cry?

### Right
There is no such thing
as the right time, but there is
a time you make right.

### Stronger
The thought of you be-
coming stronger without me
(sigh). Who's your new crutch?

### Singular
Though it ends in "s"
happiness is not plural.
All you need is you.

### Gone
Those people you thought
you needed did not "miss the
boat". They chose to walk.

### Bye
You're in or you're out
and if you're out your opini-
on does not get in.

# Kimism

I'm done with trying to make you like me.

If I'm not your cup of tea pick another flavor.

KimBMiller.com

38

# Mom, Gone
# Too Soon

I am love
The first lips that touched your face were mine
I watched you breathe
I thought you knew I had to go
I was only meant to be a temporary guardian of your heart
I can't stay
You must walk without me
Focus on our love
Pain can't erase what we have
Don't let my death kill you
I love seeing you prosper
You make me proud
Death is not a sentence
It's a word
Remember the love, fun, dreams we made together
You can still do them
I'll be looking
Making sure you keep your promises
Live for me
Live for you
Make Mother's Day, purpose day
Don't you use me to stay stagnant
I birthed a conqueror
I saw it in your eyes
You are not wrong for missing me
Just don't miss your own life too
I'm at peace
I want you to find a piece of peace too

I'll always love you

Mom

# Haiku

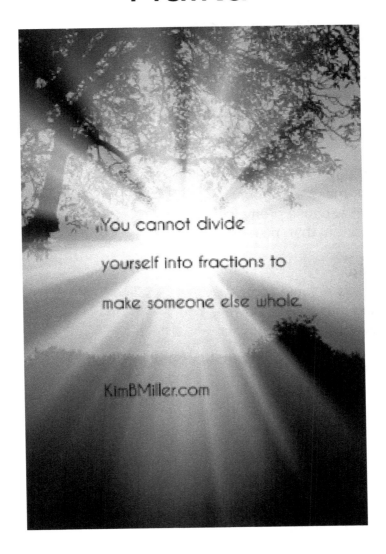

You cannot divide

yourself into fractions to

make someone else whole.

KimBMiller.com

## Haiku (continued)

### Time
Reclaiming my time!
Your time to waste does not in-
clude my time to give.

### Power
You were looking for
someone powerful. I just
showed you your mirror.

### Makeup
Your makeup is your
blanket cause pretty is more
important than pain.

### Keep
Love is not just some-
thing that you give away. You
have to keep it too.

### Define
Stop asking people
who can't write to define you.
Your blood is not ink!

### Happy
If everybody
is happy but you then no-
body is happy.

# Kimism

Moments
Others
Missed

Thank you for being there for me.

KimBMiller.com

# Poetry Is

Remember when you thought words had to be in a melody to sing to you

Poetry was a foreign flavor, an acquired taste

You thought poems like roses are red made you well read

You didn't realize poetry has blossomed

I don't blame you

Poetry is often unrecognizable

Spoken with passion and whispered

Written on hearts in invisible ink

So how can I expect you to embrace the unseen

Seen in many forms but grouped together as one

What is poetry

Poetry is unsolicited help

It holds us up when pain tries to erase our voice

It allows us to pour into emptiness and create peace

The ingredients in one poem can feed people who didn't even realize they were hungry

Poets make feelings tangible

They script mountains into pebbles

Poetic verses feel the wind caressing every syllable

Some poems rhyme, no reason

They almost have a subtle fragrance

An undeniable scent that is unexpected but welcomed

This garden of poets is stunning and diverse

Each poet's pen bleeds an alternate personal truth

So don't judge an ink by its color

There are no rules

The lines in paper are just suggestions

Besides a poet's words ascend from the limitation of paper

They make tears flow

They break stereotypes

Poems are medicinal and poetry is freedom exhaling

Words are not owned, we all just borrow them

Poetry is rented words meant to make a permanent change

The next time you inhale the aroma of a poem

Feel the words and embrace the energy they provide

Embrace unconfinable art drawn with words

Poetry is expression, floured in feelings

It can be a moment or a life time of moments

What is poetry

Poetry is the first time you kissed words and words kissed you back

# Haiku

*Haiku*

Stop arguing with

people and go ahead and

"do you" while they talk.

*KimBMiller.com*

48

## Haiku (continued)

### Haiku
Ink drops at a deep
pitch, only poets can hear.
Truth needs a partner.

### Greatness
Be who you are, not
to impress but to inspire.
Let your greatness drip.

### Judge
You need to stop giv-
ing people the pen and pa-
per to judge you with!

### Pens
You understand that
poets write about pain they
didn't walk through too. Right?

### Pay Poets
Poets are not acces-
sories. Expose them to
cash not excuses.

### Crumbs
If you are satis-
fied with crumbs, why would they of-
fer you a whole meal.

# Kimism

*If your dreams don't scare you....*

# Dream bigger!

*KimBMiller.com*

# The System

I am not broken

I am drained

The ocean is washing pain into my fragile soul

I am bleeding from separation

From family

From people whose blood runs through my pain

As I play life I wonder which family domino will fall next

Knocking down another as they are tipped into obscurity

Swimming with one stroke

Holding on by a thread

I look for answers to why

Why aren't you here

Why aren't I enough

Why am I stuck in a system that causes more problems than it solves

Why is innocence placed in homes while the guilty go free

Issues float to the surface

This water is muddied with pain

Separation is not drowning

Float until your consciousness appears before you

We're all in the water

Clinging to our own baggage, dripping biases

Open your ears to another perspective

Compassion is your life jacket

Empathy is your air

Why keep adding tears to an ocean of agony

Blame infused in opinions

Fear hidden in truth

I feel invisible; I live in between their blinks

Hidden from view

My family with broken pieces is still a family

Division does not subtract love

No more shame

No more silent truths

No more hiding

Secrets can't hide

Every drop of truth should feel like a hug and taste like promises

Don't add seasoning

Truth is best served raw with a side of integrity

They could not rescue me

They can't even swim themselves

# Haiku

Haiku


Believe silence. When
people do not answer you,
they did answer you.


KimBMiller.com

## Haiku (continued)

### Reflect
You hated your re-
flection and blamed the one who
made you their mirror.

### Which One
Think! Are you looking
for a reason to leave or
a reason to stay?

### Currency
If truth was used as
a currency many of
you would still be broke.

### Educate
He might not have a
degree but that doesn't mean he
can't educate you.

### Quote
You quote singers but
you don't quote yourself. Puppets
don't always have strings.

### Script
When did your pain turn
into background noise to a
script you did not write?

# Kimism

Love yourself

enough

to know

you are enough.

KimBMiller.com

# Fear

I slipped away

I dropped fear off

I don't think it needs me

I was always polite

I made it feel comfortable

But I'm sick of the sofa bed

It's not comfortable

I don't know how I was so unbothered

No pre-existing excuses were planted in my indecisiveness

This is my garden

I only planted non-confrontational seeds

I just felt like using genetically modified reasons

I think, I mean I know

I escaped though

I'm good now

If, scratch that I meant to say when…

When I slipped away I……

I mean you can't just drop fear off and be okay

Right

I needed a plan for my plan to follow

So I could stay focused while looking away

You know how hard it is to say goodbye

Goodbyes are not my problem

It's the loss of a flavor that used to dominate every meal

That's what I miss

It's like pre-seasoned defeat

But that doesn't matter now

I'm not going back

Do you think I should go back

I'm just kidding

I don't need fear

I can get so much done now

I've eradicated my restriction

No more fear

I wonder what fear is doing

Maybe I should…

No

I am not going back

Not this time

I have a right to a life

Fear looks at me and says: Are you done rehearsing

I say: Yes

It must be time to eat

What's on the menu

Defeat with roasted promises on a bed of lies

Served with an empty glass of opportunities

# Haiku

Haiku

No one can tell you
to get back in your lane if
you own the highway.

KimBMiller.com

## Haiku (continued)

### Win
Fear, doubt and haters
can only win if you give
them the victory.

### Out
Fear and doubt cannot
be drowned out by using some-
one else's theme song.

### Drink
Ain't you sick of gar-
gling with someone else's spit.
Drink your own Kool-Aid.

### Fact
True fact: if you lis-
ten to a lie long enough
it becomes your truth.

### Get Back
If you cannot do
it, don't correct those who can.
Get back in your cave.

### Light
Don't let this darkness,
make you forget that you were
born to be a light.

# Kimism

KimBMiller.com

Just Do More

# More Haiku

# Think About It

### Shadow
You're walking behind
someone who can't lead you. No
one needs two shadows.

### More
How did they become
more important than you? You
gave them permission.

### Peace
The power you give
their validation is hurt-
ing you. Peace can't breathe.

### Likes
Yes, they threw likes at
your post but they don't like you.
Jealousy likes you.

### Why
How come "Super" is
a man but we have to "Won-
der" about woman?

# Traditional Haiku

**Butterflies**
Butterflies can't swim.
So, they dance with large rain drops.
Music is dripping.

**Trees**
The thin trees drank rain.
Drops of sunshine on the grass.
Rain's tears screamed catch me.

**Wind**
Wind carries a scent.
A flower's fragrance can't hide.
Nature's free perfume.

**Clouds**
Clouds form like pillows.
Lightning interrupts their sleep.
Darkness fights the light.

**Lake**
Frozen lakes form fun.
Winter's breath is blowing joy.
We glide 'till frost bites.

# Less Talk

### The Game Life
Some of you talk a-
bout life because you're "board" and
got no game, talk less.

### Some
Some people talk "a
good game" because they actu-
ally can't play one.

### King
Stop quoting King when
you act like Hitler. Fake words
do not make you real.

### Chadwick
Chadwick had real Black
Panthers. Your folks spill your tea
before you sip it.

### Lie
The shoe fits. Are you
talking about me? Yes, Cin-
der-lie-a, I am!

# Relationships

### Two Jobs
If as soon as you
lose your job she leaves... Well then,
now you lost two jobs.

### No Job
Companionship is
not a solution to pain.
Don't give love a job.

### Baggage
Stop blaming men for
having baggage when you have
a storage unit.

### Level
Ciara didn't know
she had the wrong Future till
she started Russeling.

### Bye Bye
Him: You ain't nothing!
Me: I was nothing that's why
I picked you. Bye, boy!

## Misc.

### Mirror
Some of you do not
have haters, unless your mir-
ror started talking.

### Past
That was my past, so
why do you keep bringing it
up. Old dirt, same you!

### Can't Drown
When that wave of pain
comes, don't forget you can swim.
Can't drown standing up.

### Media
Stop letting medi-
a sound bites decide what you
should chew on. Go read!

### Math
Math ain't hard. Divi-
sion can multiply hate, if
you add ignorance.

# Explained- Normally, I don't explain my haiku but for these five I will.

## Lemonade
Beyonce made some
lemonade, but some of you
should not have drank it.

> **Explanation**: Beyonce has a phenomenal visual, musical album called Lemonade. When it came out I noticed several people were distancing themselves from people who had not watched it. Yes, enjoy all of her "dopeness" but don't belittle people who don't feel the same way.

## Soul
Aretha taught soul
lessons but some of you did
not report to class.

> **Explanation**: Aretha is known as the Queen of Soul. Her sound is distinctive. If you are going to try to sing one of her songs make sure you are "soul" talented.

## Chapter
If you're helping some-
one, help them. Facebook don't need
to know that chapter.

> **Explanation:** Stop posting, each and every time you help someone. Just help the person who needs help.

## Wisdom
Stop asking fools for
wisdom. You don't see lions
asking sheep nothing!

> **Explanation:** Lions are the king of the jungle.
> They don't ask sheep what to do because they
> are kings. We need to do the same. Stop
> asking fools for wisdom. They cannot help you.


## Go Write
Stop trying to write
non-"friction" poems and write your
truth. Whispers don't scream.

> **Explanation:** Stop trying to write nonabrasive
> poems. If you are writing about something that
> is "ugly" or combative then that's what it is.
> Don't feel the need to write pretty poems about
> ugly things.

CPSIA information can be obtained
at www.ICGtesting.com
Printed in the USA
FSHW020140241220
76949FS